olive oil

olive oil

sauces, appetizers, & entrées

RYLAND
PETERS
& SMALL
LONDON NEW YORK

Designer Iona Hoyle
Senior Editor Clare Double
Picture Research Emily Westlake
Production Manager Patricia Harrington
Publishing Director Alison Starling

First published in the United States in 2007
by Ryland Peters & Small
519 Broadway, 5th Floor
New York, NY 10012
www.rylandpeters.com

10 9 8 7 6 5 4 3 2 1

ISBN-10: 1-84597-393-3
ISBN-13: 978-1-84597-393-3

Printed and bound in China

Notes
All spoon measurements are level unless
otherwise stated. Eggs are large unless
otherwise specified. Uncooked or partially
cooked eggs should not be served to the very
old, frail, young children, pregnant women, or
those with compromised immune systems.

Ovens should be preheated to the specified
temperature. Recipes in this book were tested
with a regular oven. If using a convection oven,
decrease the temperature by 40°F, or follow the
manufacturer's instructions.

contents

introduction 6
appetizers & little dishes 14
entrées 30
dressings & sauces 52
index & conversion chart 62
credits 64

a cultural icon

A bottle of really superb, estate-bottled, cold-pressed, extra virgin olive oil may cost more than the equivalent amount of champagne, since it takes about ten pounds of olives to make just four cups of this wonderful substance. But it is worth every penny. Olive oil is a nutritional marvel as well as a gastronomic joy. It keeps its distinctive, complex flavor and aroma and stays chemically intact because it contains health-giving nutrients such as tocopherol (vitamin E) to keep it stable. It is excellent for general cooking, and even for frying, since it doesn't degrade during prolonged use at high temperatures.

For well over two millennia, olive trees, their fruit, and their oil have been integral to the culture and eating habits of the Mediterranean—at the heart of Western culture. In fact olives and civilization have almost become synonymous. *Olea europaea*, the cultivated olive, has now spread to California, South Africa, Chile, Argentina, Australia, New Zealand, and, surprisingly, China, but the myth of its "Mediterranean" nature endures.

Today olive oil is one of the world's biggest health stories. We know that olive oil has revolutionary properties, mainly linked to its high levels of monounsaturated fatty acids, which could guard against arterial heart disease. In addition, because of its antioxidant properties, it can reduce free-radical damage in cells and therefore minimize the effects of aging, and even protect against cancer.

making olive oil

It is reassuring to know that olive oil can be made from the pressed juices of the olive and nothing else, by law. In Italy and France, Spain and Portugal, many of the traditional terraced slopes and groves are now uneconomical to run, although prestigious regions in these countries, such as Liguria, Tuscany, Sardinia, and Provence, still thrive. Spain and Greece continue to supply the market with large quantities of excellent extra virgin and virgin olive oils (some of which are blended to a degree of uniformity for the mass market). Increasingly, much production is being relocated to other Mediterranean sites such as Turkey and Tunisia, where the wage demands are lower and seasonal harvest workers more readily available, as are grants from EU sources.

The Harvest

By late fall and early winter, the olives are green, succulent, and perfect for early-picked oil. Later, the fully ripe, purplish, dark-brown fruits will yield quite a different oil. Fully ripe olives produce the most oil and are therefore more profitable, but many believe the best oil is from green-ripe fruit because as they ripen, olives damage more easily and can fall and bruise, sustaining enzyme and oxidation damage that affects the taste.

Ideally, fruit to be pressed for oil should be picked by hand. This requires skill, patience, and the absence of autumnal gales; olive picking is not only tricky but physically tiring. The fruit must be clean and free of twigs and leaves before crushing, and ideally reaches the pressing house, then is processed, within 36 hours. On small estates this is possible, but at a large plant there may be many olives from different sources waiting to be treated. They can become affected by the heat as they stand, which may compromise quality and flavor.

Extracting the Oil

Methods of extracting the oil vary from age-old and labor-intensive means to industrial centrifuging processes that traditionalists feel harm the taste and chemical structure of the oil. There are also intermediate methods including extraction using a centrifuge operating at gentler speeds, a rapid process popular with some producers. Finally there is filtering, tasting, blending, grading, bottling, labeling, and packaging.

grades and names

About a tenth of world production is top-class virgin oil, the purest form, of which there are four designated grades. The remainder is refined to remove flaws or impurities. Some of this refined olive oil is blended with virgin oils to create "olive oil"; this tastes less good and is cheaper, but it is consistent and useful in its own right. The international olive oil trade grades oils on their amount of free acidity (which should be small) and on their smell and taste. They may also be chemically analysed to detect any unacceptable substances in the oil. Descriptions from the producer, such as "first, cold-pressed," "estate bottled," or "unfiltered" can help you assess quality and style. Words such as "lite" or "light" are not official terms and so may be misleading.

Virgin olive oil

Any oil obtained solely from the olive by mechanical or other physical methods, under thermal conditions that do not cause any alteration of the oil. The only processes permitted are washing, extraction, decanting, centrifuging, and filtering. The use of solvents is not permitted.

Extra virgin olive oil

Virgin oil of perfect aroma and flavor and of no more than 1 percent free acidity. Many "commercial" extra virgin olive oils are skillfully blended to a standard maintained from year to year, and to a price. They may come from different regions and countries. "Single estate" products are often superb unblended oils, more expensive, and pronounced in flavor.

Virgin olive oil/fine olive oil

Virgin oil with a perfect aroma or flavor, but with free acidity of up to 2 percent.

Ordinary/semi-fine virgin olive oil

Virgin oil of good but not perfect taste and aroma and with free acidity levels of up to 3.3 percent.

Refined olive oil

Refined from virgin oils (generally lampantes) by processes which, by law, must not alter the oil's initial glyceride structure.

Olive oil/pure olive oil

Specific foodstuff terms used on a label to mean a blend of refined olive and virgin olive oil. Suitable for frying and general cooking where Mediterranean distinctiveness is not required.

what's on the label

First, cold-pressed
The very first pressing, with little or no heat applied. A superb product retaining its natural distinctiveness; often expensive.

Cold-pressed
Simply extracted without any heat above 82°F, but perhaps from the second pressing of the same olives. Still a good product, keeping many healthy qualities and flavor.

Estate-bottled/single estate
Top quality, premium-price oils, often from hand-picked olives and cold-pressed within hours of picking. Probably from one family estate or farm, it is grown, extracted, and packaged on home ground. The Americas, Australia, New Zealand, and even South Africa, as well as the great oil-producing areas of Europe, produce these oils.

Affiorato/flor de aceite/lágrima
Also called "flowers" or "tears". This is "free run" oil—the olives will often have been coarsely crushed, but not pressed: the oil merely runs off and is collected. This is rare and very desirable.

Date and year of pressing
Aim for oil as young as possible. Very new oil may be pungently bitter, but this softens within several months. No oil lasts well for more than a year.

Unfiltered
Means one less process and implies excellent oil and careful handling. Often murky, it is described as "veiled," since "cloudy" would imply a fault.

Single varietals/blends
The producer has used only one variety of olive, or a blend.

Designation of origin
Refers to oils from specific zones or regions that safeguard local traditions and olive types. In Spain it is called DO, in Greece PGI or PPO, in Italy DOC.

Organic/ecological production
Many small-scale oil producers and some cooperatives cultivate olives using organic methods approved by certified agencies.

Selecting olive oil
Choose a first cold-pressed or *affiorato* oil to trickle over food at the table. Cold-pressed, extra virgin oils (one peppery, one mellow) are useful for salads, pasta, soups, and dressings. Keep cheaper extra virgin olive oil for general cooking and an ordinary virgin olive oil for mayonnaises and baking. "Olive oil" (a blend of refined and virgin) can be used for frying or bulk baking.

appetizers & little dishes

caponata

1 eggplant, about 10 oz., cut into ½-inch cubes

1 tablespoon salt

¼ cup extra virgin olive oil

2 red onions, each cut in 8 wedges

4 garlic cloves, chopped

1 cup dry-cured green olives

¾ cup dry-cured black olives

⅓ cup capers in salt

2 teaspoons chopped fresh oregano or thyme leaves, plus extra sprigs, to serve (optional)

3 tomatoes, each cut in 8 wedges

2 baby zucchini, sliced crosswise

2 tablespoons tomato paste

2 teaspoons sugar

⅔ cup chicken or vegetable stock or water

¼ cup chopped, fresh, flat-leaf parsley, to serve

serves 6–8

This colorful dish is a classic Italian antipasto and comes from Sicily. It is also delicious with grilled fish or steak. Caponata may be served warm, cool, or cold, but not chilled.

Sprinkle the eggplant with the salt, toss well, and let stand for 10 minutes. Drain and pat dry with paper towels.

Put the oil in a large heavy saucepan and heat until very hot. Add the onions, garlic, olives, and capers. Stir over high heat for 2–3 minutes, then add the eggplant and continue to cook, stirring, over medium heat for another 8 minutes. Using a slotted spoon, transfer the mixture to a plate and set aside.

Add the oregano or thyme to the pan, then add the tomatoes, zucchini, tomato paste, sugar, and stock or water. Stir gently and bring to a boil. Reduce the heat and simmer for 8 minutes. Return the eggplant mixture to the pan and simmer gently until the flavors have mingled. The vegetables should still be intact, not mushy. Dip the pan into a bowl of cold water to cool.

To serve, transfer to a bowl, sprinkle with parsley, and top with the extra sprigs of oregano or thyme, if using.

panzanella

3-4 thick slices crusty country bread, torn into pieces

2 red bell peppers, seeded and cut into quarters

2 yellow bell peppers, seeded and cut into quarters

3 medium ripe, red, juicy tomatoes

3-4 garlic cloves, crushed to a purée

$\frac{1}{3}$-$\frac{1}{2}$ cup extra virgin olive oil

1 tablespoon red wine vinegar

2 teaspoons balsamic vinegar

6 anchovy fillets, halved lengthwise

6 caperberries or 2 tablespoons salted capers

a small bunch of basil

a few celery leaves (optional)

serves 4-6

A great summery or autumnal appetizer, this Tuscan dish has been interpreted worldwide. It needs superb, ripe, flavorful ingredients, so make it whenever you have wonderful sweet peppers, tomatoes, and fresh, bouncy basil leaves.

Cut or pull the bread into 1-inch chunks or smaller, and either leave plain or toast briefly under a preheated broiler or on a grill.

Cook the red and yellow bell peppers under a hot broiler until the skins blister. Remove the skins and reserve the flesh. To prepare the tomatoes, cut a cross in the bottom, dip them into a saucepan of boiling water for about 30 seconds, then remove and pull off the skins. Put the tomatoes into a strainer set over a bowl to catch the juices. Cut or tear the tomatoes in half, then remove them and discard the seeds.

Cut the tomatoes into smaller pieces and put into the bowl of juice. Add the garlic, oil, and two vinegars, and stir to make a dressing.

Put the anchovies and caperberries into a bowl, cover with boiling water, let soak for 5 minutes, then drain, reserving the liquid.

Put the bread, tomatoes, peppers, caperberries, anchovies, and half the basil into a bowl. Pour over the dressing and enough of the caperberry-anchovy soaking liquid to give a good flavor.

Toss gently and let stand for 10-20 minutes. Top with the reserved basil and celery leaves, if using, and serve.

bagna cauda

½ cup unsalted butter, melted

6–8 garlic cloves, well crushed

⅓ cup extra virgin olive oil

4 oz. canned anchovy fillets, drained, chopped, and mashed

your choice of:

red, yellow, or orange bell peppers, seeded and cut into 8 wedges

celery stalks

Belgian endive • Treviso

inner leaves from romaine lettuce

scallions • baby asparagus

cauliflower florets

broccoli florets, quartered lengthwise

fennel bulbs, cut into wedges lengthwise

sprigs of flat-leaf parsley

serves 4–8

This intensely flavorful Italian dip is made with olive oil, although it may also be made with butter, particularly in the north. This version combines both methods, and speeds the process wonderfully. Amazingly, the result is mellow and smooth, not aggressively pungent at all. The crisp, sweet, mild vegetables offset the salty flavor of the sauce.

Put the butter and garlic into a nonstick skillet and heat gently, until the butter has melted. Transfer to a blender and add the olive oil and anchovies. Purée for 2–3 minutes, then transfer to a serving bowl. The bowl of dip should be kept hot over a low candle flame.

Surround the hot dip with the cold, crisp vegetables and serve.

Note The traditional method is to put the butter and puréed garlic into a shallow terracotta dish and stir for 5–10 minutes over low to medium heat. Add the anchovy fillets and mash over the heat. Add the oil, reheat gently, then serve as above.

goat cheese marinated in olive oil

1 lb. goat cheese, sliced and quartered

2½ cups virgin olive oil

½ cup pitted black olives (optional)

4 garlic cloves

a selection of:

1 small red chile, 2–3 sprigs of fresh thyme or rosemary, 2 bay leaves, and 1 tablespoon peppercorns

lemon peel

sea salt

makes two ½-pint jars

Marinate your own goat cheese in olive oil—it can then be used broiled on toast, as a pasta sauce with snipped herbs, or served with a selection of crisp crackers.

Put the goat cheese in 2 sterilized Mason jars (see below). Pour in the olive oil, add salt, then push in the olives, if using. Blanch the garlic, your selection of herbs and spices, and the lemon peel in boiling water for 1 minute, drain, then add to the jar.

Cover and leave to marinate in the refrigerator for 2 days before using within 1 week.

Sterilization of preserving jars Wash the jars in hot, soapy water and rinse in boiling water. Place in a large saucepan and then cover with hot water. With the lid on, bring the water to a boil and continue boiling for 15 minutes. Turn off the heat, then leave the jars in the hot water until just before they are to be filled. Invert the jars onto a clean kitchen towel to dry. Sterilize the lids for 5 minutes, by boiling, or according to the manufacturer's instructions.

olive oil and garlic bruschetta

4 large garlic cloves

⅓ cup extra virgin olive oil

a good pinch chile flakes

¼ cup chopped fresh parsley (optional)

for the bruschetta:

4 thick slices country bread, preferably sourdough

extra virgin olive oil, for sprinkling

serves 4

This is pared-down simplicity and so easy to make. It beats the likes of doughballs and garlic bread hands down. The most important thing is not to overcook the garlic—it must on no account turn brown. This is great served instead of garlic bread with a selection of salads.

Slice the garlic lengthwise into paper-thin slices. Heat a small pan, pour in the olive oil, and stir in the garlic. Cook until the garlic starts to give off its aroma and is golden but not brown (or it will taste bitter). Remove from the heat, then mix in the chile flakes and parsley, if using. Cover to keep warm.

To make the bruschetta, broil, toast, or pan-grill the bread on both sides until lightly browned or toasted, then sprinkle with olive oil. Spoon or brush over the garlicky chile oil and eat immediately.

moroccan-style marinated black olives

3 cups black olives in brine

2 tablespoons fennel or cumin seeds, crushed

1 tablespoon green cardamom pods, crushed

1 tablespoon small, hot, dried red chiles

2 tablespoons allspice berries, crushed

3–4 cups extra virgin olive oil

8-inch strip of orange zest, bruised

12 fresh bay leaves, washed, dried, and bruised

makes one large 6-cup jar or three 2-cup jars

Black olives that have already been cured will mellow even more if you crack them a little or prick them with a fork, then marinate in spices and fine olive oil. Experiment until you find a flavor you like—your own customized blend. This is an aromatic Moroccan-inspired version; you could even use Moroccan olive oil for an authentic result.

Rinse the olives in cold water, drain, then pat dry with paper towels. Put them on a clean, dry surface and crush them lightly with a meat hammer or rolling pin, or prick with a fork, to open the flesh a little.

Put the fennel seeds, cardamom, chiles, and allspice in a dry skillet and toast over a moderate heat for a few minutes until aromatic.

Put the olive oil in a saucepan and heat to 350°F—a cube of bread should turn golden-brown in 40–50 seconds. Let cool a little. Using a sterilized spoon, pack the zest, bay leaves, olives, and spices into a clean jar (see below) in layers. Cover with the hot olive oil. Let cool, uncovered. When cold, seal and store in a cool, dark place.

Leave for at least 1 week before tasting. These olives keep well and improve for some months.

Note See page 20 for information on sterilizing preserving jars.

focaccia with olives

1 package (2¼ teaspoons)
active dry yeast

2 cups all-purpose flour, plus
¼ cup for shaping

½ teaspoon sea salt flakes

2 tablespoons extra virgin olive
oil, preferably Italian

topping:

finely shredded zest of 1 orange

grated zest and freshly squeezed
juice of 1 orange

½ cup extra virgin olive oil

2 garlic cloves, crushed

2 tablespoons fresh rosemary
leaves, coarsely chopped

½ teaspoon coarsely crushed
black pepper

1 teaspoon sea salt flakes
or crystals

1 cup dry-cured black olives

serves 4

This focaccia dough is a quick food processor version with olive oil in the topping and the dough. This is practical and delicious, since there is no need to rub the flour in. You could use lemon instead of orange, oregano rather than rosemary, or other toppings such as anchovy-stuffed green olives.

Put the yeast, flour, and sea salt into a food processor fitted with a plastic blade. Pulse briefly to sift the ingredients. Mix the oil and ⅔ cup warm water and, with the machine running, pour it in all at once through the feed tube. Process, in short bursts, for 15 seconds until a soft mass forms (not a ball). It will be sticky and soft.

Scoop out the dough. Add the extra ¼ cup flour as you knead and thump the dough for 2 minutes. Put the ball of dough into an oiled bowl and enclose the bowl in a large plastic bag. Leave in a warm place until the dough has doubled in size, about 50 minutes.

Pat and stretch the dough into a rectangle about 10 x 8 inches. Transfer to an oiled oven tray. Prod the dough all over with your fingertips to form dimples to take the topping.

Mix the orange zests and juice, oil, garlic, rosemary, pepper, and half the salt, and pour over the dough. Sprinkle with the olives, pushing well into the dimples. Set aside for 30 minutes to rest the dough.

Bake in a preheated oven at 400°F for 25–30 minutes or until crusty and aromatic. Sprinkle with the remaining salt. Cut into generous squares, then serve hot or warm.

rosemary, raisin, and olive oil bread

1 tablespoon dried active yeast

3 tablespoons sugar

3 cups plain flour, warmed (but not hot)

2 large sprigs fresh rosemary, washed and dried

6 tablespoons extra virgin olive oil

1 cup raisins or dried muscatel grapes

makes 6 rolls

These rosemary-flavored buns were traditionally eaten in Italy on Maundy Thursday. The olive oil is essential for a good flavor, so use the best. Raisins are traditional, but chopped ready-to-eat figs make a delicious alternative.

Dissolve the yeast and 1 teaspoon of the sugar in 1 cup warm water and leave to stand for 10 minutes until frothy.

Sift the flour into a bowl, add the remaining sugar, then make a well in the center and add the yeast liquid. Mix until it comes together, then knead on a lightly floured work surface for 10 minutes until elastic. Put the dough in a clean bowl, cover with plastic wrap and leave to rise in a warm place for about 1½ hours.

Meanwhile, strip off the rosemary leaves and lightly bruise them with the end of a rolling pin. Heat them with 4 tablespoons of the olive oil in a small pan. Remove from the heat and cool. Strain when cold.

Uncover the dough and knock it back. Tip out onto the work surface and knead in the cooled olive oil and rosemary with the raisins. Pull the dough into 6, shape into balls, then put on a floured baking sheet and flatten slightly. Using a very sharp knife, make two cuts along the top of each roll, then two across, like a grid. Cover and leave in a warm place for 30–40 minutes until doubled in size.

Uncover and brush with the remaining olive oil. Bake in a preheated oven at 350°F for 30 minutes until risen and brown, and the rolls sound hollow when tapped on the bottom.

creamy tomato and bread soup with basil oil

1½ quarts vegetable, chicken, or meat stock

¼ cup olive oil

1 onion, chopped

2½ lb. very ripe, soft tomatoes, coarsely chopped

10 oz. stale white bread, thinly sliced, crusts removed (or bread crumbs)

3 garlic cloves, crushed

1¼ cups freshly grated Parmesan cheese, plus extra to serve

sea salt and freshly ground black pepper

basil oil:

⅓ cup freshly chopped basil

⅔ cup extra virgin olive oil

serves 6

For this comforting soup you need great tomatoes, good bread, and wonderful, green olive oil. The leftover bread thickens this rich tomato soup, which is in turn enriched with Parmesan. In Tuscany, where this dish comes from, you would be given olive oil at the table to pour over the soup yourself, but here basil oil is used instead.

Heat the stock slowly in a large saucepan. Meanwhile, heat the oil in a second large saucepan, add the onion and tomatoes, and sauté over gentle heat for about 10 minutes until soft. Push the mixture through a food mill or strainer, and stir into the hot broth. Add the bread and garlic.

Cover and simmer gently for about 45 minutes until thick and creamy, beating from time to time to break up the bread. Take care, because this soup can catch on the bottom.

Meanwhile, to make the basil oil, put the basil and olive oil in a blender and blend until completely smooth—if not, pour through a fine strainer.

To finish, stir the Parmesan into the soup, then add salt and pepper to taste. Ladle into bowls and trickle 2 tablespoons basil oil over each serving. Serve hot, warm, or cold (not chilled), with more Parmesan.

creamy wheat and bean soup with rosemary

1¼ cups dried borlotti beans

½ cup dried chickpeas

a pinch of baking soda

6 tablespoons extra virgin olive oil, plus extra to drizzle

2 garlic cloves, finely chopped

2 tablespoons chopped fresh rosemary

1 tablespoon tomato paste diluted with ½ cup warm water

1½ cups Italian farro or whole spelt grains

sea salt and freshly ground black pepper

serves 6

Italian farro is a very ancient grain, cultivated by the Romans until wheat overtook it in popularity. It is a close relation of the grain spelt, which makes a good alternative. Cooked with beans, it makes a creamy, nutty soup, delicious served with thick slices of country bread.

Soak the beans and the chickpeas overnight in abundant cold water. Drain, then cook with a pinch of baking soda in a large pan of boiling water for 45 minutes to 1 hour until tender. Drain, reserving 2 quarts of the cooking water. Mash the beans a little to start them disintegrating, then set aside.

Heat the oil in a medium saucepan and add the garlic and rosemary. Cook for 1 minute until the garlic turns light golden and the rosemary releases its fragrance. Add the diluted tomato paste, then pour in the reserved cooking water. Bring to a boil, then stir in the farro. Season with salt and pepper and simmer gently for 1 hour or until the farro is al dente.

Stir in the lightly mashed bean mixture. Taste and adjust the seasoning, being generous with the pepper. Reheat, adding extra water if the soup is too thick. Serve in large bowls with extra virgin olive oil to drizzle over the top.

mozzarella, tomato, and arugula salad

3 x 5 oz. buffalo
mozzarella cheeses

4 large, juicy, ripe red tomatoes

4 large handfuls of arugula,
about 3 cups

about ½ cup first-pressed extra
virgin olive oil

sea salt and freshly ground
black pepper

serves 4

The famous Italian *caprese* salad normally includes basil.
In this variation, arugula adds a peppery bite. Find milky, soft
buffalo mozzarella, which has a better flavor than the cows'
milk version. Add ripe, flavorful tomatoes and an exceptional
extra virgin olive oil, and this dish becomes sublime. Eat it
immediately, and never refrigerate this salad.

Drain the mozzarellas. Slice thickly or pull them apart into big rough
chunks, showing the grainy strands. Arrange down one side of a
large serving platter.

Slice the tomatoes thickly and arrange them in a second line down
the middle of the plate. If the slices are very large, halve them. Add
the arugula leaves down the other side of the platter.

Sprinkle with salt and pepper, then just before serving trickle the
olive oil over the top. Make sure you have some crusty bread
(slightly char-grilled tastes good) to mop up the juices.

salad of wild greens

2 handfuls peppery leaves, such as arugula or watercress

2 handfuls bitter leaves, such as chicory, escarole, or frisée

2 handfuls crisp green lettuce, such as baby romaine, torn

1 small head Belgian endive, separated into leaves

1 small head radicchio, separated into leaves

leaves from 1 small bunch of flat-leaf parsley, dill, or mint (optional)

1 small red onion

dressing:

2 garlic cloves, crushed

½ teaspoon sea salt flakes

1–1½ tablespoons freshly squeezed lemon juice

⅓–½ cup extra virgin olive oil, preferably Greek or Italian

serves 4

In Greece and Italy wonderful selections of baby green leaves and herbs are gathered from gardens and fields in spring and summer, from wild samphire to dandelion greens, arugula, wild mustard, curly endive, purslane, radish, and beet leaves. The ingredients here are guidelines for you to assemble your own wild salad.

To make the dressing, put the garlic, salt, and half the lemon juice in a small bowl and mix with a stick blender. Drizzle in the oil and blend until a rich emulsion forms. Taste, then add enough lemon juice to give bite.

Alternatively, use a mortar and pestle to pound the garlic and salt to a sticky paste. Drizzle in the oil, continuing to pound and stir until a rich emulsion forms. Add lemon juice to taste.

Wash the leaves and herbs, if using. Finely slice the onion into rings. Put the leaves, herbs, and onion rings in a large bowl. Cover with a plastic bag, seal, and chill until ready to serve, so the leaves stay crisp and fresh.

Just before serving, trickle the dressing over the leaves and toss thoroughly with your hands or 2 wooden spoons.

spanish roasted vegetable salad

2 red bell peppers

2 yellow bell peppers

½ butternut squash or
1 lb. pumpkin, unpeeled

2 red onions, unpeeled

2 Spanish onions, unpeeled

½ cup extra virgin olive oil,
preferably Spanish

4 medium-sized,
vine-ripened tomatoes

sea salt and freshly ground
black pepper

serves 4–6

A classic Spanish dish full of sweet summer bounty. It can be served hot, warm, or cool, and is especially good accompanied by country bread and a lively Spanish wine such as Rioja or Rosado.

Cut the bell peppers in half lengthwise, slicing through the stems. Leave these intact but discard the pith and seeds.

Slice the squash or pumpkin into 1-inch disks or chunks.

Cut all the onions crosswise into halves, leaving the roots and tops intact. Leave the skins on too—they give extra color and flavor and protect the shape.

Put the peppers, squash or pumpkin, and onions, cut sides up, in a large, lightly oiled roasting pan. Drizzle half the oil over the vegetables and sprinkle with sea salt and pepper.

Roast near the top of a preheated oven at 475°F for 30 minutes, until the vegetables are frizzled, wrinkled, and soft. Add the tomatoes for the last 10 minutes of cooking time.

Drizzle the remaining oil over the top and serve hot, warm, or cool. Eat the salad with your fingers, discarding the skins, roots, and stems along the way. This is superb with bread to scoop up the sweet, oily, sticky juices from the hot pan.

stewed fennel with olive oil, lemon, and chile

4 medium heads of fennel

1 cup extra virgin olive oil

finely grated zest and freshly squeezed juice of 1 large unwaxed lemon

1 anchovy in oil or salt, rinsed and finely chopped

½ teaspoon hot red pepper flakes

a little white wine vinegar (optional)

sea salt and freshly ground black pepper

serves 4–6

In this dish, the fennel absorbs all the flavors of the olive oil, lemon juice, and chile, and the anchovy adds a salty touch. Braising the fennel slowly makes it meltingly soft and tender. This is delicious with pork and robust fish like swordfish, and can be made in advance; it only improves with keeping and is better the next day.

Trim the stalks and fronds from the fennel. Discard the stalks, but keep the green fronds. Halve the fennel bulbs. Cut out the hard core, then cut each half into 2 wedges. Arrange the fennel wedges in a flameproof baking dish.

Put the olive oil, lemon zest and juice, anchovy, pepper flakes, vinegar, if using, salt, and pepper in a bowl and whisk well. Pour over the fennel. Bring the dish to a boil on top of the stove. Cover with foil and bake in a preheated oven at 325°F for 1 hour or until very soft and tender.

Remove from the oven and remove the foil. Taste the liquid and add a dash of vinegar to sharpen it if necessary. Serve warm or cold, sprinkled with the reserved fennel fronds.

ratatouille

2 lb. eggplant, cut into pieces

extra virgin olive oil (see method)

2 medium onions, coarsely chopped

2 red bell peppers, 2 yellow bell peppers, and 1 green bell pepper, halved, seeded, and cut into pieces

6 small zucchini, about 1½ lb., halved lengthwise and sliced

4 garlic cloves, crushed

6 medium tomatoes, halved, seeded, and chopped

a small bunch of basil, coarsely chopped

coarse sea salt

to serve:

a few basil leaves, finely sliced

1 garlic clove, crushed

serves 4–6

To make this ratatouille, you add each vegetable separately, in the order that best suits its cooking requirements. Each vegetable "layer" must be seasoned individually. Cut the pieces medium-large, about 1½ inches thick, to keep the flavors distinct from each other. Serve with crusty bread.

Put the eggplant pieces and 3 tablespoons water in a microwave-proof bowl. Microwave on HIGH for 6 minutes, drain, and set aside.

Heat 3 tablespoons oil in a deep sauté pan with a lid. Add the onions and cook until soft, 3–5 minutes. Salt lightly.

Add all the bell peppers and cook for 5–8 minutes more, stirring often. Turn up the heat to keep the sizzling sound going, but take care not to let it burn. Salt lightly.

Add 1 more tablespoon oil and the zucchini. Mix well and cook for about 5 minutes more, stirring occasionally. Salt lightly.

Add 2 more tablespoons oil and the drained eggplant. Cook, stirring often, for 5 minutes more. Salt lightly.

Add the garlic and cook for 1 minute. Add the tomatoes and basil plus 1 more tablespoon oil if necessary, and stir well. Salt lightly. Cook for 5 minutes, then cover, lower the heat, and simmer gently for 30 minutes, checking occasionally.

Remove from the heat. Serve at room temperature, stirring in extra basil and garlic just before serving.

bell peppers stuffed with pasta and tomatoes

4 medium yellow or red
bell peppers

2 oz. very fine spaghetti

⅓ cup extra virgin olive oil

12 ripe cherry tomatoes,
quartered

2 garlic cloves, finely chopped

¼ cup chopped fresh basil

½ cup pine nuts, coarsely chopped

1 cup freshly grated pecorino
cheese

½ teaspoon dried red hot pepper
flakes (optional)

sea salt and freshly ground
black pepper

serves 4

These roast bell peppers are a vegetable and pasta course in one. They should be luscious and soft, with a wrinkled, browned exterior. The garlicky cherry tomatoes keep the pasta moist, and the chile and pecorino give a hint of sharpness. This is a good accompaniment for fish.

Slice the tops off the bell peppers and reserve. Scrape out and discard all the seeds and white pith. Set the peppers upright in a lightly oiled dish small enough to fit them snugly. If they don't stand upright, shave a little piece off the base, but not right through.

Cook the pasta in plenty of boiling salted water until just al dente, about 8 minutes or according to the package instructions. Drain well and toss with 2 tablespoons of the olive oil.

Put the tomatoes in a bowl with another 2 tablespoons of oil, the garlic, basil, pine nuts, pecorino, and pepper flakes, if using, and mix well. Add the pasta to the peppers, filling them by two-thirds, then spoon in the tomato mixture. Put the pepper lids on top and brush liberally all over with the remaining olive oil.

Bake in a preheated oven at 425°F for 25–30 minutes or until the peppers start to wrinkle and blister. Serve hot or at room temperature.

chicken with tomatoes, garlic, and olives

2 tablespoons extra virgin olive oil

1 free-range chicken, about 4 lb., cut into 6-8 pieces

8 garlic cloves, finely chopped

2 cups canned chopped tomatoes

a pinch of sugar

⅓ cup black olives, preferably niçoise, pitted and coarsely chopped

a bunch of fresh basil, torn

coarse sea salt and freshly ground black pepper

serves 4-6

This hearty chicken dish is found all over France, but the southeastern version here has particularly assertive flavors. It goes well with rice or fresh pasta, such as the saffron tagliatelle pictured here.

Heat 1 tablespoon of the oil in a large sauté pan. Add the chicken pieces and brown on all sides. Transfer the chicken to a plate, salt generously, and set aside. Add the remaining oil and garlic and cook for 1 minute; do not let it burn. Add the tomatoes and sugar. Stir well and return the chicken pieces to the pan. Cover and simmer gently until the chicken is cooked, 25–30 minutes.

Transfer the chicken pieces to a serving dish, then raise the heat and cook the sauce to thicken slightly, about 10 minutes. Add salt and pepper to taste, then stir in the olives. Pour the sauce over the chicken pieces, sprinkle with the basil, and serve immediately.

greek chicken stifado

1 free-range chicken, about
3 lb., whole or quartered, or
4 breast or leg portions

2 tablespoons extra virgin olive oil

10 whole cloves

20 pearl onions or
10 shallots, halved

8 small potatoes, quartered

4 garlic cloves, chopped

2 tablespoons white wine vinegar
or lemon juice

⅓ cup rich tomato paste
(double strength)

14 oz. canned chopped tomatoes

24 black olives, such as Kalamata

a large bunch fresh or dried
rosemary, oregano, thyme,
or a mixture

freshly ground black pepper

serves 4

In Greece *stifado* can refer to a number of things, but essentially it is a thickened stew with tomato, garlic, and olive oil—perfect for winter. Sometimes made with beef or rabbit, guinea fowl, or even quail, it is a handsome dish, easy to prepare, and fragrant with herbs. Serve from the dish, accompanied by torn country bread, noodles, or rice.

Pat the chicken dry with paper towels. Heat the olive oil in a large flameproof casserole dish, add the chicken, and sauté for 8–10 minutes, turning it with tongs from time to time.

Push the cloves into some of the onions and add them all to the pan. Add the potatoes, garlic, vinegar, tomato paste, tomatoes, olives, and freshly ground black pepper. Tuck in the herb sprigs around the edges.

Bring to a boil and reduce the heat to low. Cover and simmer for 30 minutes for chicken pieces, or about 60 minutes for a whole bird—until the chicken seems tender and the sauce has reduced and thickened.

provençal beef daube with lemon and parsley

2 lb. beef round steak, cut 1 inch thick

2 tablespoons extra virgin olive oil

10 garlic cloves, sliced

8 oz. slab bacon, cubed

2 red onions, quartered

4 medium carrots, left whole

6 plum tomatoes, cut into wedges

1 unwaxed lemon and grated zest

1 fresh bouquet garni of thyme, bay, parsley, and oregano

¾ cup prunes

1 cup rich red wine

¾ cup boiling beef stock

a bunch of flat-leaf parsley, freshly chopped

⅓ cup fresh brioche or bread crumbs (optional)

sea salt and freshly ground black pepper

serves 4

This is a simplified version of a classic stew, left bubbling for hours, enriched with bacon, and fragrant with red wine. It's straightforward, so there's time to make the aromatic lemon, parsley, and garlic topping, gremolata (which is not Provençal, but Italian). The lemon adds extra vibrancy to the dish. Like most stews, this will improve over several days.

Beat the beef all over with a meat hammer or rolling pin, then cut it into 2-inch square chunks. Heat the oil in a large flameproof casserole dish, add the beef, in batches if necessary, and sauté for 4 minutes on each side. Remove with a slotted spoon and set aside.

Add 2 of the garlic cloves to the pan, then add the bacon, onions, and carrots. Stir and sauté until the bacon is golden and the fat has run. Add the tomatoes, half the lemon zest, the bouquet garni, prunes, wine, and stock. Replace the browned beef, pushing the pieces well down under the liquid.

Remove the white pith from the lemon. Cut the flesh into tiny cubes and add to the pan, to give flavor and tenderness to the meat.

Reduce the heat to a gentle simmer. Cover with a lid and cook, undisturbed, for 1½ hours, then test for doneness. (If preferred, cook in a low oven at 325°F for 2½ hours or until tender.)

To make the gremolata, chop the remaining garlic, and mix with the remaining lemon zest, the parsley, and bread crumbs, if using. Serve the daube with its sauce and the gremolata sprinkled on top.

dressings & sauces

hummus

1 cup dried chickpeas (if possible, without skins), or 2 cups cooked

freshly squeezed juice of 1 lemon

2 garlic cloves, crushed

¼ teaspoon salt

2 tablespoons tahini paste (optional)

½ cup first-pressing extra virgin olive oil

freshly ground black pepper

to serve:

hot paprika

extra virgin olive oil

makes 2 cups

Fresh, lemony hummus makes a delicious snack—add the sesame richness of tahini to give a more intense effect. Excellent olive oil utterly defines the flavor: use a beauty. For 10-minute hummus, use canned chickpeas.

If using dried chickpeas, put them in a bowl and cover with boiling water for 3 hours (or in cold water for 8 hours). Drain. Put in a large saucepan, cover with boiling water, bring to a boil, partially cover, and simmer for 1½–2½ hours or until the chickpeas are easily crushable and tender. Drain.

Put the chickpeas in a food processor with the lemon juice, garlic, salt, pepper, and the tahini paste, if using. Blend briefly to a mousse. With the machine running, drizzle the oil through the feed tube to form a creamy purée. Season to taste.

Serve cool or chilled, sprinkled with a little hot red paprika and with the traditional trickle of extra virgin olive oil. Accompany with crisp lettuce leaves and heated, torn or cut flatbreads as well as other crisp raw vegetables.

classic vinaigrette

¼ cup white or red wine vinegar

1¼ cups extra virgin olive oil

sea salt and freshly ground white pepper

makes 1½ cups

The simplest olive oil dressing is a drizzle of best-quality extra virgin oil, followed by a few drops of aged balsamic vinegar. This classic vinaigrette is an emulsion of oil and vinegar with, if you wish, seasonings such as mustard.

Put all the ingredients in a bowl, vinaigrette flask, or screwtop jar. Whisk, beat, or shake to form a temporary emulsion. Store in a cool, dark place, since rancidity can occur in bright sunlight and heat. Use within a week—and shake again to mix before use.

To make a smaller amount—enough for one salad—use 1 part vinegar to 5 parts oil, plus seasoning to taste. If preferred, pour the ingredients into the base of the salad bowl and beat them with a fork. Put the salad on top and leave undisturbed (no longer than about 30 minutes), then toss just before serving.

mustard vinaigrette

Add 1 tablespoon hot dry mustard or mixed mustard such as Dijon. This will create a stable emulsion and add bite.

lemon and anchovy vinaigrette

Use lemon juice instead of vinegar. Pound 6 canned anchovy fillets with the pepper and some of the lemon juice. Add about 2 tablespoons tiny pickled capers and mix with the oil.

simple mayonnaise

2 egg yolks, at room temperature

2 teaspoons Dijon mustard

¼ teaspoon salt

2 teaspoons freshly squeezed
lemon juice or white wine vinegar

¾ cup extra virgin olive oil

⅔ cup light oil, such as grapeseed,
safflower, or sunflower oil

makes 1⅔ cups

Egg yolks, with a little acidity and seasoning, at the right temperature and degree of agitation, have the miraculous ability to absorb huge volumes of oil to form a rich, thick emulsion and this classic sauce. Many find olive oil alone too intense a taste, so here it is blended with a lighter oil.

Put the egg yolks into a medium bowl with high, straight sides and a curved base. Stir in the mustard, salt, and half the lemon juice and beat until smooth.

Mix the oils in a small pitcher then, with the oil pitcher in one hand and an electric, hand-held whisk in the other, gradually drizzle the oil into the egg yolks, whisking continuously to form a stiff, glossy emulsion. When all the oil has been added, taste, then whisk or beat in the remaining lemon juice. Taste and adjust the seasoning. Cover the surface with plastic wrap until ready to use. Best used immediately, mayonnaise may also be refrigerated for up to 3 days.

aioli

Pound the salt with 4 garlic cloves to form a sticky paste, beat in the eggs, then proceed as in the main recipe.

tarragon mayonnaise

Use tarragon vinegar and add 2 teaspoons blanched, chopped tarragon leaves to the finished mayonnaise. This is superb with chicken, poached fish, and eggs.

classic pesto

100 g pine nuts

½ cup extra virgin olive oil

6 garlic cloves, chopped

1 teaspoon coarse sea salt
or rock salt

1 cup fresh basil leaves, torn

½ cup freshly grated Parmesan
cheese

½ cup freshly grated pecorino
cheese

makes about 3 cups

Italy calls it pesto, France calls it pistou—but this family of sauces is always a mixture of fresh herbs blended to a paste with garlic, salt, and good olive oil. Basil is traditional, but good sauces can be made with parsley or arugula, while cilantro gives it a Middle Eastern or Asian flavor. Most contain cheeses and some include nuts, usually pine nuts.

Put the pine nuts in a small skillet, add 1 teaspoon of the olive oil, and stir-fry quickly until golden. Remove and let cool.

Put the pine nuts, garlic, salt, and basil in a food processor and work to a paste. Alternatively, use a mortar and pestle. Still working, add half the cheese, then gradually pour in half the olive oil. Add the remaining cheese and oil all at once and work or blend one last time. The paste should be a vivid green.

cilantro pesto

Use half parsley and half cilantro instead of the basil. Use almonds in place of pine nuts and use all Parmesan, not a mixture.

arugula pesto

Replace half the basil with arugula; this gives a bitter edge that tastes curiously good.

black olive paste

3 cups dry-cured black olives

2 tablespoons capers, rinsed

8 canned anchovy fillets, rinsed and chopped

½ teaspoon freshly ground black pepper

1 teaspoon dried oregano, marjoram, or thyme

1 small, hot chile pepper, finely chopped, or 1 garlic clove, chopped (optional)

⅓ cup extra virgin olive oil

to serve:

carta da musica, *grissini* (Italian breadsticks), or other flatbreads

1–2 tablespoons extra virgin olive oil

serves 4–6

This paste is pungently delicious and makes a perfect appetizer. It is traditionally served with a Sardinian flatbread, *carta da musica*, which is often dried into crisp, brittle round sheets, but breadsticks or another flatbread make good substitutes.

If you are serving the paste with flatbreads, brush one side with 1–2 tablespoons of olive oil. Transfer to a preheated oven and bake at 400°F for 8–10 minutes, then turn off the oven and leave the door slightly ajar.

To make the paste, pit the olives. Put the olives into a food processor, then add the capers, anchovies, pepper, dried herb, and chile or garlic, if using.

Chop the mixture in several short, pulsing bursts. With the machine running, slowly pour in the oil through the feed tube, until the mixture forms a rich, coarse purée. Don't overprocess: some contrast in texture is important.

Serve the olive paste with the hot flatbreads. The paste may be stored in the refrigerator for up to 2 weeks.

index

a
anchovies
    bagna cauda 19
    black olive paste 60
arugula: mozzarella, tomato, and arugula salad 35

b
bagna cauda 19
basil: creamy tomato and bread soup with basil oil 31
beef: Provençal beef daube with lemon and parsley 51
borlotti beans: creamy wheat and bean soup with rosemary 32
breads
    black olive paste 60
    creamy tomato and bread soup with basil oil 31
    focaccia with olives 27

olive oil and garlic bruschetta 23
    panzanella 16
    rosemary, raisin, and olive oil bread 28
butternut squash: Spanish roasted vegetable salad 39

c
caponata 15
cheese
    goat cheese marinated in olive oil 20
    mozzarella, tomato, and arugula salad 35
chicken
    chicken with tomatoes, garlic, and olives 47
    Greek chicken 48
chickpeas: hummus 53
chile: stewed fennel with olive oil, lemon, and chile 40

e
eggplant
    caponata 15
    ratatouille 43

f
farro: creamy wheat and bean soup with rosemary 32
fennel: stewed fennel with olive oil, lemon, and chile 40
focaccia with olives 27

g
garlic
    chicken with tomatoes, garlic, and olives 47
    olive oil and garlic bruschetta 23
goat cheese marinated in olive oil 20
greens: salad of wild greens 36

h
herbs: classic pesto 58
hummus 53

l
lemons
    Provençal beef daube with lemon and parsley 51
    stewed fennel with olive oil, lemon, and chile 40

m
mayonnaise, simple 57
mozzarella, tomato, and arugula salad 35

o
olive oil
    grades and names 11
    labels 12
    making 9
    olive oil and garlic bruschetta 23
    rosemary, raisin, and olive oil bread 28
    stewed fennel with olive oil, lemon, and chile 40
olives
    black olive paste 60
    chicken with tomatoes, garlic, and olives 47
    focaccia with olives 27
    Moroccan-style marinated black olives 24

p
panzanella 16
parsley: Provençal beef daube with lemon and parsley 51
pasta: bell peppers stuffed with pasta and tomatoes 44
peppers
    bell peppers stuffed with pasta and tomatoes 44
    panzanella 16

ratatouille 43
Spanish roasted vegetable salad 39
pesto, classic 58
potatoes: Greek chicken *stifado* 48
pumpkin: Spanish roasted vegetable
salad 39

r
ratatouille 43
rosemary
creamy wheat and bean soup with
rosemary 32
rosemary, raisin, and olive oil
bread 28

s
salads
mozzarella, tomato, and arugula
salad 35
salad of wild greens 36
Spanish roasted vegetable salad 39
soups
creamy tomato and bread soup
with basil oil 31
creamy wheat and bean soup with
rosemary 32

t
tomatoes
bell peppers stuffed with pasta
and tomatoes 44
chicken with tomatoes, garlic, and
olives 47
creamy tomato and bread soup
with basil oil 31
Greek chicken *stifado* 48
mozzarella, tomato, and arugula
salad 35
panzanella 16
ratatouille 43
Spanish roasted vegetable salad 39

v
vinaigrette, classic 54

conversion chart

Weights and measures have been rounded up
or down slightly to make measuring easier.

Oven temperatures:

°C	°F	Gas
110°C	(225°F)	Gas ¼
120°C	(250°F)	Gas ½
140°C	(275°F)	Gas 1
150°C	(300°F)	Gas 2
160°C	(325°F)	Gas 3
180°C	(350°F)	Gas 4
190°C	(375°F)	Gas 5
200°C	(400°F)	Gas 6
220°C	(425°F)	Gas 7
230°C	(450°F)	Gas 8
240°C	(475°F)	Gas 9

Volume equivalents:

American	Metric	Imperial
1 teaspoon	5 ml	
1 tablespoon	15 ml	
¼ cup	60 ml	2 fl.oz.
⅓ cup	75 ml	2½ fl.oz.
½ cup	125 ml	4 fl.oz.
⅔ cup	150 ml	5 fl.oz. (¼ pint)
¾ cup	175 ml	6 fl.oz.
1 cup	250 ml	8 fl.oz.

Measurements:

Inches	cm
¼ inch	5 mm
½ inch	1 cm
¾ inch	1.5 cm
1 inch	2.5 cm
2 inches	5 cm
3 inches	7 cm
4 inches	10 cm
5 inches	12 cm
6 inches	15 cm
7 inches	18 cm
8 inches	20 cm
9 inches	23 cm
10 inches	25 cm
11 inches	28 cm
12 inches	30 cm

Weight equivalents:

Imperial	Metric
1 oz.	25 g
2 oz.	50 g
3 oz.	75 g
4 oz.	25 g
5 oz.	50 g
6 oz.	75 g
7 oz.	200 g
8 oz. (½ lb.)	250 g
9 oz.	275 g
10 oz.	300 g
11 oz.	325 g
12 oz.	375 g
13 oz.	400 g
14 oz.	425 g
15 oz.	475 g
16 oz. (1 lb.)	500 g
2 lb.	1 kg

credits